Riviera Style

Publisher Beatrice Vincenzini
Executive Director David Shannon
Editorial Director Alexandra Black
Art Director David Mackintosh
Publishing Assistant Charlotte Wilton-Steer

First published in the UK by Scriptum Editions
Created by Co & Bear Productions (UK) Ltd.

Printed and bound in Novara, Italy by
Officine Grafiche de Agostini.

First edition
10 9 8 7 6 5 4 3 2 1

ISBN 1-902686012

Riviera Style

WRITTEN BY DIANE BERGER

PHOTOGRAPHY BY TIM CLINCH
AND FRANCESCO VENTURI

SCRIPTUM EDITIONS
LONDON · HONG KONG

Contents

FRENCH GLAMOUR

› The Côte d'Azur ‹

French Glamour

When French socialite Madame De Sévigné first visited the Côte d'Azur in the late eighteenth century, she noted in her diary "… that never has there been a landscape so beautiful or delicious." She was not the first to be so tantalised, and certainly not the last, for the French Riviera has fascinated pleasure seekers for centuries. In modern times, wealthy Victorians were among the first to realise its potential. They, along with European and Russian aristocrats, fled to the Côte d'Azur to escape the northern winters, justifying their forays as health cures. According to William Chambers, writing in 1817, "Fashion ennui and love of gaiety seem to send quite as many abroad as absolutely bad health." By the following century, it had become clear that it was pleasure, more than anything, that was the Riviera's real attraction — for the socialites of the Roaring Twenties, for the artists and writers of the modern movement, for the movie stars of the 1950s and 1960s, and still for travellers today.

Henry, Lord Brougham, formerly Chancellor of Great Britain, was among the first prominent Englishmen to seek the solace of the Côte d'Azur. Accompanied by his daughter, he checked into a small auberge in Cannes, which although simple, had hosted celebrated guests such as French novelist Victor Hugo. It took less than a fortnight for Brougham to fall in love with the region's ambience and he immediately bought Villa Eleanore, which would be his home for many years. Once the word was out, droves of well-placed English followed suit. In 1878 the Prince of Wales sailed to the Riviera on the Britannia,

OPPOSITE & RIGHT The Riviera dream was one of carefree days spent yachting and sunbathing, and glamorous evenings of cocktail parties, candlelit dinners, dancing and roulette. The dream is captured here by bikini-clad models relaxing on deck and a tanned Lana Turner stepping out for a night in Cannes.

explaining that, "I go to the Riviera as I would a club. It's a place with good company where everyone mingles, just like a garden party."

Late-nineteenth-century pleasure seekers transformed their newly found paradise of perched villages and fishing ports by constructing fairytale castles in the belle époque style, building boulevards for promenades by the sea, and filling gardens with imported exotic plants. Fantasy and exoticism were everywhere in evidence. In the 1920s and 1930s, few embodied the pleasure principle more convincingly than wealthy American socialites Gerald and Sara Murphy. F. Scott Fitzgerald dedicated *Tender is the Night* to "Sara and Gerald Murphy – Many Fêtes". They indeed loved a good fête, or party, and their home, Villa America in Antibes, provided the backdrop for many. Describing it in his novel as the Villa Diana, Fitzgerald wrote that it was approached "by a walk marked by an intangible mist of bloom, that followed the white border stones … to a space overlooking the sea where there were lanterns asleep in the fig trees and a big table and wicker chairs and a great market umbrella from Sienna, all gathered about an enormous pine …" Inside, all was new-wave, with white-splashed walls, black tiled floors and black-satin upholstered furniture. On the terrace, which the couple used as an outdoor dining and living room, simple café tables and chairs — painted silver — replaced the usual wicker or fancy wrought-iron versions. It was in the words of the Murphy's biographer Amanda Vaill, "… fresh, eclectic, unexpected, way ahead of its time."

OPPOSITE The fairytale setting of Cannes with its lavish belle époque buildings and palm-lined beach became the perfect backdrop for Hollywood to show off its latest stars, and for couturiers to display their talents. Zsa Zsa Gabor makes a suitably glamorous statement at the 1952 Cannes Film Festival.

RIGHT Sophia Loren dresses to impress at the Cannes Film Festival in 1955; Jack Palance and Arlene Dahl outside the Carlton during the 1954 festival.

Fashion, then as now, was big on the Côte d'Azur. Coco Chanel designed her famous beach pyjamas there, with pockets large enough to hold gambling chips for the women who were succumbing to the glittering casino scene. This gave Juan-Les-Pins its playful name "Pyjama Land," and marked the beginnings of resort wear as a significant fashion force. A few decades later, Brigitte Bardot would spark an international craze for gingham after wearing a simple dress made out of it in St Tropez.

Whether designers, writers, artists, intellectuals, filmmakers or simply celebrities, there were many who fell in love with, and made their mark on the Côte d'Azur. Noel Coward composed "I went to a Marvellous Party" after one of the infamous local fêtes, and the play *Private Lives* was conceived and rehearsed in a Côte d'Azur villa. Writers as disparate as André Gide, Edith Wharton, Graham Greene, Somerset Maugham, Françoise Sagan, Colette and Jean Paul Sartre all drew on the Riviera for inspiration. The dazzling light drew artists, from Matisse to Cocteau to Picasso. The magical backdrop attracted film directors and their attendant stars. And photographers like Jacques-Henri Lartigue were on hand to capture it all.

The atmosphere of creative freedom was indicative of how journalist Mary Blume describes life on the Riviera in general. "Illusion is its chief industry … To the foreigner, the Côte d'Azur was a place of escape, escape from winter's cold and social constraints: the place to get away from it all and, eventually, to get away with everything." This very quality made the Riviera the ideal location for a film festival. The Cannes Film Festival began in 1946, but it was not until 1956 that Roger Vadim's film,

RIGHT One of the Côte d'Azur's most celebrated residents was Picasso, pictured in 1957 with wife Jacqueline at their villa in Cannes. Picasso was one of the many artists, writers and intellectuals who found creative freedom on the Riviera.

Et Dieu Créa La Femme, starring Brigitte Bardot and set in nearby St Tropez, put the festival on the map. The Côte d'Azur became the most glamorous of film-world haunts, frequented by Bardot, Grace Kelly, Audrey Hepburn and other silver-screen icons.

Hollywood delivered this brand of Riviera chic to an audience of millions, in films like *To Catch a Thief* and *Monaco Baby*, and soon everyone was flocking to the palm-lined strip to capture their own slice of glamour. And the beauty of places like St Tropez was that everyone could do so. Vadim described it as "… the happy mixture of old and young, wealth and class. A person with no money could live like a millionaire and a millionaire could have fun living like a bohemian."

An elderly Colette deplored the new-found popularity of her beloved Côte d'Azur, lamenting, along with others of the old guard such as Sara Murphy and Zelda Fitzgerald, that people actually had to *share* a beach. A piece of their private fantasy world had gone public. But the essential atmosphere of the Côte d'Azur has remained — in the grand soirées and grand yachts contrasted with village fêtes and painted fishing boats; in extravagant villas juxtaposed with humble fishermen's cottages; and in the most elemental of all pleasures, the sun and the sea.

RIGHT

When she set up home in St Tropez, Brigitte Bardot not only made the tiny port extremely fashionable, she also set trends with her brand of low-key resort dressing.

☽ **LEFT & BELOW RIGHT** The pool, set in a topiary garden of animal shapes, reflects Diane and Tom Berger's passion for the fantasy elements of eighteenth-century French style. Bought while on holiday in the Camargue, a Vietnamese bamboo bicycle with paniers full of fresh flowers reveals the couple's love of travel and of the village markets.

Costume Drama

Anthropologists have written for centuries that a house reflects and reveals its owners' souls and that their interests can be read through its visual imagery. In the case of Diane and Tom Berger, there were never truer words. Their love of village life — the equestrian festivals and bullfights, the all-night fêtes in the town square, the food and flower markets, the church bells, the belle époque cafes — is passionately expressed in the interior scheme, the garden, and even the setting of their dream-like home.

The two-storey house is enveloped by vineyards and olive groves and nestled in a tiny Provençal village high in the hills above the Riviera. An art historian, Diane set out to create a fantasy world, a living incarnation of the couple's favourite song, "La Vie En Rose". In doing so, she transformed a ruin of a house with mud floors, inhabited only by scorpions, into a theatrical environment in which the furniture and decorative objects function as stage sets. Each of these sets reflects regional traditions and style, with each of the elements lovingly sourced from marches aux puces, or flea markets, architectural salvage yards and local brocante, or bric-à-brac dealers.

The house is entered through a large formal hall, its walls lined with large, trumeaux-style mirrors lit by candles. This is Diane's Provençal answer to the Hall of Mirrors at Versailles — executed in rustic style, so that the solid beams above,

☽ RIGHT & OPPOSITE Despite being a ruin when the Bergers first found it, the house has been transformed to combine the raw energy and colour of French village life with sophisticated references to art historical styles. Period wrought-iron sun loungers covered in toile de Jouy are redolent of the great age of ocean travel.

and the lavender field and topiary garden outside — the latter replete with sculpted ducks, birds and rabbits — are reflected. But it is the dining room, kitchen and outdoor eating arbour that most embody the village life that the couple wanted to make their own. In these three spaces Diane has essentially created a private bistro-café

The centrepiece of the dining room is a real butcher's table, complete with sculpted bulls' heads on the base, which Diane painted pink, then stencilled with golden dancing bulls. One wall supports a screen retrieved from an old bistro, adorned with images of musicians and revellers, while a feature wall is covered with images of turn-of-the-century bistro paraphernalia. This delightful document provides a blueprint for the café-style kitchen, where the walls are blanketed with vintage *publicité*. Bar and shelves display a collection of classic bistro wares. One special find was a period zinc bar, replete with sink and taps, from a real café.

The master bedroom is the Bergers' vision of a Provençal dream, decorated to capture the feel of living over a village restaurant. The corona that tops the bed was found in a flea market, as was the bed itself, now draped in *bouties*. All storage is in armoires and old-fashioned laundry and textile baskets. There is not a built-in cupboard anywhere in the house. The mood of this and the other unashamedly romantic rooms in the house is capped by a soundtrack of the lulling, romantic tunes of the nineteenth-century accordion player, without which this theatre would not be complete.

☾ **OPPOSITE & BELOW LEFT** A love of costume is a recurring theme. In a hallway, a trompe l'oeil coat rack is draped with a toreador's cape, while a nineteenth-century trompe l'oeil shopfront, originally a stage set, serves as a dressing room backdrop.

BELOW RIGHT Period bistro chairs with cushions covered in a local print of bull motifs, a zinc bar and original *publicité.* transform the kitchen into a villlage café.

☽ ABOVE Doors salvaged from an eighteenth-century chateau lend a sense of grandeur to the entrance hall. In the evening, candlelit mirrors reflect the delicate pastel interior colours, gilt-edged furnishings and bundles of bright sunflowers.

RIGHT The main salon is intended to bring old-world Provence to life. Unmatched period furniture, each piece covered in a different prettily patterned fabric, has been combined with antique portraits and antique sculptures. Dominating the room is a delicate Aubusson-style canvas.

◗ OPPOSITE Trompe l'oeil is used to great effect in most rooms. The stairwell is lined with panels depicting a construction site in eighteenth-century Paris. They were the final purchase for the decoration of the house and seemed a fitting tribute to the dramatic restoration project that had seen a ruin returned to its original glory.

RIGHT The vibrant pinks of the dining room were inspired by the rose tones often used by designer Christian Lacroix, born in nearby Arles. The dining table was given a slick of bright fuchsia gloss and stencilled with gold bulls, while the walls were washed in soft pink. One wall is covered by a screen, which once decorated a bistro, depicting musicians and revellers.

☾ **LEFT & BELOW** The master bedroom features an antique bed and corona, found at the famed L'Isle-sur-la-Sorgue flea market. In summer the room is flooded with sunlight, while in winter the terra-cotta floors are warmed by a roaring fire. Next door, the master bathroom has been plumbed with a nineteenth-century coiffeur's table from an antique market. It is topped with a selection of favourite bath essences and scents.

Village Life

In the late nineteenth century, the French romantic novelist Guy de Maupassant sailed into the picturesque port of the tiny fishing village of St Tropez and was immediately captivated by its rustic allure. It inspired him to write *Sur l'Eau*, in which he brings the town's artless appeal to life, describing it as "… one of those charming, simple daughters of the sea, one of those modest little towns that have grown in the water like a shellfish, fed on fish and the sea air …"

Entranced like Maupassant by the pastel-hued facades of the village houses and cafés clustered along hilly cobblestone streets, the bright sunlight and the seaside setting, a string of nineteenth- and twentieth-century artists, writers and designers were drawn to live and work in St Tropez. The painter Paul Signac was utterly seduced by its charms, as were Bonnard, Matisse, Seurat and Dufy, to name just a few. Colette, the French novelist, took up residence at La Treille. Not only did she base her famous novel *La Naissance du Jour* in St Tropez, she also opened a cosmetics shop there, frequented most famously by Coco Chanel and contributing to St Tropez's ever-evolving brand of chic.

Since those early days, the sleepy fishing village has been transformed into a haven for jet-set pleasure seekers. However, the same elements that once lured literati, intellectuals and artists remain in place. They are also the visual cornerstones of the unique Hotel Byblos — the painterly combination of light and colour, the village architecture and, of course, the sea.

RIGHT & OPPOSITE The distinctive logo of the Byblos represents the abduction of Europa by Zeus and is a charming synthesis of ancient Mediterranean myth, local ceramic arts and contemporary styling. Likewise, the design of the hotel itself combines Mediterranean tradition, indigenous architecture and modern luxury.

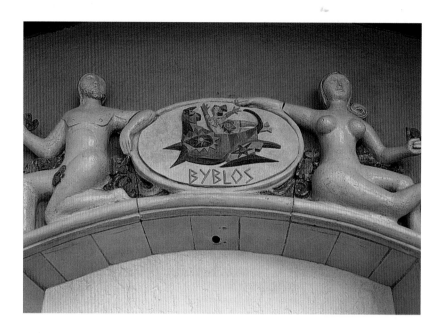

Conceived as a "village within a village", the Hotel Byblos opened in 1968 to accommodate the rich and famous who had begun flocking to St Tropez. The port had acquired new cachet in the wake of Roger Vadim's 1956 film, *Et Dieu Créa La Femme*, set in St Tropez and starring a young Brigitte Bardot, soon to become the town's most famous resident. The Byblos offered a haven of luxury and privacy that mirrored the painted village houses in architectural and decorative style — recreating and preserving the look and ambience that was the essence of the once-quaint fishing port.

Originally founded by Lebanese promoter Prosper Gay Para, the Byblos is now in the hands of French owner Aigle Azur. It was completely refurbished in 1998, but retains the flavour of a Provençal hamlet, with its painted facades and red-tiled roofs, clustered around an irresistible pool. Exquisite views unfold from its terraces as well as from the private gardens adjoining many of the luxuriously appointed bedrooms.

Although the exteriors are in traditional St Tropez style, the original owner wanted the Byblos interiors to be distinct from those of any other hotel. He created an environment rich with textures and images recalling the ancient world, using Greek, Roman and Iranian mosaics, antique marble and stone, classical sculptures and busts. The Byblos is filled with Mediterranean influences, set in a maze of narrow winding streets and private courtyards, bordered by villa-style rooms, fronted in gleaming shades of yellow, red and lavender, and surrounded by a sea of olive trees, oleander and swaying palms.

OPPOSITE & ABOVE The bright plaster facades were designed to blend in with the old town of St Tropez. To add dynamism, the original interior decorator, André Denis, employed ceramicist Roger Capron to create the bas-relief overlooking the pool, the striking paved floor of the patio and the hotel logo itself.

BELOW & OPPOSITE An appealing mix of local colour and gracious living defines the Byblos. This ethos extends to the bar, which showcases regional ceramic craftsmanship in the form of the hotel logo designed by Roger Capron. Details such as the mix-and-match Provençal-style chairs on the poolside dining terrace and the Byblos's own label cuvée, are all part of the mood of laid-back luxury.

OPPOSITE The peach-coloured exterior of this rustic house in a charming cobblestone street was inspired by local facades. It is a few minutes' walk away from the market and the harbour in one of the Côte d'Azur's chicest villages.

Summer Sojourn

The Italian owners of this bijou village house, in one of the French Riviera's most stylish and sought-after harbourside resorts, came here looking for a cross-cultural experience. They wanted to enjoy the best of Italy during the winter months and the attractions of the Côte d'Azur during the summer. After spending holidays in hotels for two seasons, they were convinced they should buy a place of their own. They had already fallen in love with the location and they adored the pleasures of village life — strolls along the waterfront, lingering over coffee in cafés, shopping at the produce market. Now they just had to find the right house.

A friend of the couple finally found what they had spent months looking for — a traditional village house set in a narrow cobbled street, just a few minutes' walk from the tiny port. It was a complete wreck, consisting of little more than a facade, exterior walls and a roof, but they knew it was perfect. They bought it immediately because they could instantly visualise its potential and wanted to grab it before anyone else could. A builder was engaged straightaway and briefed on how many rooms the owners wanted and what size they should be. In less than a year, the house was habitable.

While the builder got on with the task of constructing the interior spaces, the owners worked alongside him, decorating each room to capture in material form the essential esprit and joie de vivre that they wanted to infuse their summer home.

RIGHT & OPPOSITE Bought as a complete wreck, the house has been lovingly restored by its owners, paying special attention to original architectural details such as the arched door surround, œil de bœuf windows and terra-cotta roof tiles.

The idea was that the house should convey the spirit of the village and be as typical as possible, in both its configuration and its interior scheme, of the region in which it was set. For convenience sake, many of the furnishings were bought in Italy and shipped to France. But to give it the real stamp of its native setting they added local finds sourced from antique shops and flea markets, creating a wonderful medley of Italian and French styles.

The facade, with its œil de bœuf windows and rustic shutters, was restored to look as though it had always been that way. After many attempts to get just the right paint colour for the exterior walls, they settled on a dusky shade of peach, very indigenous to the locale and symbolic of their passion for the nearby fruit and vegetable markets, where peaches figure prominently throughout the summer months.

In addition to regular forays to the local markets to stock up on fresh fruit and vegetables, wedges of fragrant cheese, loaves of aromatic breads and armfuls of herbs and flowers, summer days are whiled away at cafés and restaurants, exploring nearby villages or indulging in a favourite Italian pastime, the evening *passeggiata*, or stroll. The couple also keep a tiny Boston whaler moored in the port, conveniently at hand should they want a break from their most delightful of daily routines.

🦌 **LEFT & ABOVE** The cosy drawing room is a melange of furniture and objects bought in Italy and France, set against a simple backdrop of pale yellow walls and terra-cotta-paved floor. To maximise the small space, the staircase leads directly from the room, dispensing with a separate hallway and enclosed stairwell.

🦌 **OPPOSITE & ABOVE LEFT** A mix of French period detail and rusticated elements creates an appealing look that is both stylish and relaxed. In a small dining corner, an antique table and chairs have been given a wash of pale paint, then rubbed back — to reveal the wood below — and details picked out in gold. They create a delightful setting for charming seafood plates, delicate wine glasses and classic silverware.

ABOVE RIGHT Trips to the produce markets nearby are a daily event. Baskets of cut flowers, bundles of fresh herbs and delicious breads, cheeses and pastries all find their way onto the dining table for breakfasts and impromptu late-afternoon lunches.

✷ **OPPOSITE & BELOW RIGHT** Architect Jacques Couëlle has created an extraordinary cave-dwelling, Riviera style, for this site overlooking the Mediterranean. Its molten, flowing forms and primitive feel provide an apt backdrop for the owners' collection of modern sculpture.

Primitive Forms

Architect Jacques Couëlle had a natural affinity with the rocky curves, grottoes and cliffs of the Riviera coastline. They fit perfectly within his philosophical vision of humankind returning to its cave-dwelling roots. He wanted to create habitats that would return modern men and women to the molten, sculptural feel of the caves they once inhabited, and to produce buildings in synergy with their natural settings. This vision lies at the heart of an extraordinary house in the Baie de Cannes, designed by Couëlle in 1973.

The current owners had experienced the architect's unique view of design and living style while on holiday at the Cala di Volpe Hotel in Sardinia. A luxury resort developed by the Agha Khan and conceived by architect Jacques Couëlle, it springs from the island like an organic rock formation, a fluid, living sculpture. The couple were so taken by this enigmatic place that they commissioned Couëlle to execute their own such sculpture on the Côte d'Azur.

By this time at the height of his career, Couëlle had developed a fully formed concept for his unique brand of organic architecture. He set about realising his ideas on the clifftop site purchased by the owners, high above the bustle of Cannes. Like other projects the architect had conceived, the house was to be a "floating environment" that was rooted to the land but seemed to be suspended in space. It was to be elegant, but so married to the landscape that it appeared almost invisible.

✴ **LEFT & OPPOSITE** Better than any museum setting, the Couëlle house boasts sweeping organic forms and a bold interplay of light and shadow that provide a natural showcase for sculpture. A primitive figurine is displayed in a niche framing an exquisite sea view, while a colonnaded walkway is the setting for a collection of vases, inspired by ancient amphora and made by local potters.

Couëlle, like all the artists who were attracted to the Côte d'Azur, was fascinated by light and the way it changed the mood and appearance of the interior of a house as it ran its course from morning till evening. The interaction between natural and artificial light was also an important consideration, along with the impact of both light sources on the inhabitant's perception of space, furniture and objets d'art. This is evident in the house at Baie de Cannes, which is sited to capture and filter the changing strengths of the sun throughout the day — illuminating the stuccoed free-forms and fluid arches that delineate the interior space and drawing attention to the breathtaking sea views that punctuate the exterior walls.

The owners found themselves caught up in the spirit of Couëlle's vision, and began to collect artworks and local crafts that would complement the structural beauty of their new home. They acquired everything from canvases by Yves Kline and pots by Jean Maret, a good friend and contemporary of Picasso, to Etruscan-inspired vases by Tomek, which are at once classical and contemporary. These objects still decorate the house, which today appears just as avant-garde as it did in 1973. At the same time, however — in keeping with Couëlle's intention — its organic, sculptural qualities make it appear at one with its environment, as if it had slowly evolved from the ground over the course of centuries.

✴ **LEFT & BELOW** The primitive, almost timeless quality of Couëlle's vision allows the owners to mix objects and furnishings from different eras with no apparent conflict. In the large drawing room, an antique grandfather clock and the gold cherub suspended above seem perfectly at home.

✸ **LEFT & BELOW** This corner of the main living room is a tribute to the regional culture and geography. Behind the curved leather-covered banquette, a wall of niches is filled with all kinds of treasured objects, from shells and sponges and rustic door keys to vivid stained glass and Neo-realist art works. Couëlle was very involved in the Neo-realist art movement of the 1920s and 1930s, counting Yves Kline among his friends, and he inspired the owners to start collecting.

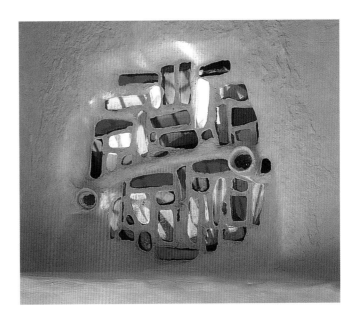

✹ OPPOSITE Couëlle has created the illusion that a lava flow has poured over the site, forming solid shapes as it cooled. His idea was to create living spaces that would put modern humans back in touch with their roots, returning them to the molten, sculptural feeling of their natural habitats as cave dwellers.

✹ LEFT & ABOVE Although niches apparently occur at random, they have been carefully thought out to be as functional as they are aesthetic. Household and decorative items can be neatly stored, eradicating the need for cupboards and enclosed storage areas. The fireplace unit provides one such example, with spaces carved out of the structure to allow for the placement of the fire itself as well for storing logs.

✳ ABOVE & OPPOSITE Fluid metalwork inspired by the regional flora adds beautiful

and delicate embellishment to the solid mass of the building with its robust forms. Gates

and stairway balustrades, both inside and out, were executed in wrought iron, bronze

and copper by local artisans. Couëlle's training under Gaudí is clearly evident in such

an imaginative and organic approach to form and material.

✳ **ABOVE & RIGHT** On this clifftop site, the
architect sought a formal return to the appearance of
the primitive grottoes of the Riviera coast. He wanted the
house to grow out of the landscape, in the same way
that grottoes seem to grow out of the sea.

🐐 OPPOSITE The main guest bedroom epitomises the purity of style that defines the entire house. A crisp white piqué bedspread, the simple curves of a wrought-iron chair and the geometry of a Biedermeir-style chest create a timeless rural harmony.

White Magic

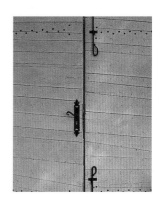

A set of white crackle-glaze Vallauris bowls from the 1930s, bought at an English country house sale some twenty years ago, was the unlikely catalyst drawing two Britons to the wooded hills behind St Tropez. The Vallauris bowls, which take their name from the famous pottery town near Antibes, had belonged to Lady Portarlington, a stylish hostess who had taken a number of houses on the Côte d'Azur, furnishing them herself with enormous taste and charm. Simplicity was her leitmotiv — uncluttered, but comfortable rooms, curtains and coverings made from plain local fabrics and a mix of the old and new. Although the bowls themselves were soon forgotten, packed away in a cupboard, their purchase clearly marked the owners' first yearnings for a house of their own in the south of France.

Many years later, friends offered to lend them a house in a hamlet not far from St Tropez, set amidst a patchwork of vineyards, lavender fields and woods of oak and chestnut trees. After three summers spent in this idyllic retreat, the house was put on the market. It seemed madness to buy it but, given their deep attachment to the place, even madder not to. At the eleventh hour, contracts were signed, and since then there has been no looking back.

The property comprises a main house and two guest cottages, all built of the local pierre de Bormes.

LEFT Every attempt has been made to bring a sense of the outdoors inside. French doors and windows open onto a fragrant garden and poolside terrace with glimpses of the sea visible on the horizon. Panama hats are always at the ready for ventures outside.

OPPOSITE A Provençal cherrywood table serves as a sideboard in the summer and a dining table in the winter, when it is too cool for evening meals outdoors. A Vallauris bowl takes pride of place on the table.

Approaching from the lane that passes through the hamlet, one is only aware of a long stone wall and a pair of wooden doors, with the name of the house, L'Olivaie, an old French word for olive grove, carved in stone above. Only on opening the doors is the magic of the house and garden revealed. From the terrace with its pergola covered in wisteria and solanum, the eye is led down first to a formal level with a stone *bassin* and box hedges and then on to a lower, more informal area. There, silvery olive trees underplanted with collages of thyme, geranium and cistus provide a framework for the garden. Clipped box and pittosporum add architectural detail, while the whites of the roses and oleander, the blues of the plumbago and agapanthus, and the greys of teucrium and helichrysum give tonality of colour.

Much of the inspiration for the decoration inside the house came from the owners' great friend and taste mentor, Walter Lees. The key throughout is simplicity, the interest coming from the mixing together of objects. In the salon, which sets the mood for the rest of the house, a comfortable sofa and chair are covered in white piqué, the curtains are white cotton from the local market and on the floor are white geometric rugs from the renowned factory in Cogolin, so often used by London interior designer David Hicks. On the walls hang contemporary pictures which marry well with charming pieces of eighteenth-century French country furniture. Most importantly, taking pride of place on a long Provençal table in the salon, are the white Vallauris bowls, which have now come to settle, like its owners, in their spiritual home.

ABOVE & OPPOSITE Throughout the house pristine white walls and furnishings are brought to life by the use of carefully selected fabrics and painted woodwork in the hallmark colours of the south of France: lavender blue, almond green or turtle-dove grey. A colourful antique bedspread hanging over the balustrade and Piranesi prints on the walls set off the stairwell of the main house, while a guest bedroom is simple, yet comfortable, with crisp white linens on the bed.

LEFT & ABOVE The bijou kitchen reflects regional style, with local tiles in deep blue conjuring up the mood of the sea. As the owners love to entertain, this small room is a constant hub of activity, especially in the summer months when the house is filled with guests. Although the kitchen is designed for function, rustic baskets, locally crafted earthenware and wire drying racks add charm even to the sink area.

OPPOSITE & BELOW During the summer, lunch is served under the pergola, often after an aperitif of Vin d'Orange, made in the winter from the orange trees that grow in tubs on the terrace. The table is set with local Biot glass, pottery from Vallauris and monogrammed napkins bearing the name of the house, L'Olivaie. Local dishes feature strongly, such as soupe au pistou, gratin de courgettes and tomates Provençale.

☿ OPPOSITE & BELOW RIGHT Classical Greek sculpture and motifs of maritime culture are a common feature of Villa Kérylos — emblematic of original owner Théodore Reinach's passion for archaeology and ancient civilisation.

Grecian Lore

During the late nineteenth century, it was the vogue for people of immense wealth to construct follies, or fantasy villas, inspired by historic monuments or exotic places. Most of these fairytale concoctions were drawn almost entirely from the imagination, but Kérylos, La Villa Grecque, in Beaulieu-sur-mer is a very different story. Impeccably researched and executed by its archaeologist-owner, Théodore Reinach, it is a tribute to Hellenistic Greek design.

Not only did Reinach admire the architecture, interior decoration, furniture and art of the ancient civilisations whose scholarly study he made his life, he also harboured a deep affinity with the aesthetic and philosophical foundations of classical culture. Inspired by Greek temples, which were open to the sea and sky, he chose a site on the tip of the Baie des Fourmis. Surrounded by the Mediterranean on three sides, the villa would appear to be at one with the water and would capture changes in the piercing Riviera sunlight throughout the day.

Reinach hired the like-minded architect Emmanuel Pontremoli, a native Niçois, to help bring his dream to fruition. The villa had to offer unlimited views from every perspective and allow the natural light to play out dramatic themes on interior volumes, frescoes and mosaics. The blueprint that evolved from this idea was inspired by the city of Delos and resulted in the villa's

☿ **LEFT & OPPOSITE** Mosaics are an integral part of the interior scheme at Villa Kérylos. Most depict mythological scenes from ancient Greek lore, incorporating marine motifs such as shells, seahorses and waves. These are evocative not only of antiquity but also of the villa's waterside setting.

arrangement around an open, peristyle courtyard. The interiors, meanwhile, integrated influences from Ancient Rome, Pompeii and Egypt. Once Reinach had carefully looked over and approved the plans for the villa and its interior scheme, work began in 1902, taking six years to complete.

The furniture was commissioned from the cabinetmaker Bettenfeld, who worked from specially made drawings of ancient pieces such as thrones, chairs, tabourets and "klismos", Greek-style chairs with curved backs and legs. All of these were perfectly placed to capture unhindered views of the sea. There were even beds for reclining while dining, just as the ancients did. The villa also had to function as a home, including recently available mod-cons and bathrooms with sophisticated plumbing. But even this was carried out in antique style, with water pipes laid beneath the floor for heating, as was the custom in aristocratic Pompeiian villas. Interior decorators Adrien Karbowsky and Gustave Louis Jaulmes oversaw the execution of the decorative painting and mosaics, basing their designs on ancient Greek public buildings as well as patrician Pompeiian homes. The delicate stucco work was created by sculptor Paul Jean-Baptiste Gascq, a winner of the Grand Prix de Sculpture.

At the same time as constructing a monument to the past, Reinach was patronising the master craftsmen of his own age. On his death, he left the villa to l'Institut de France to ensure that the magical spirit of antiquity which he so revered would remain intact for the enjoyment of the public and act as a source of inspiration for generations to come.

☿ **OPPOSITE & ABOVE** The pristine environment of Villa Kérylos attracted many admirers — including neighbour Gustave Eiffel, Gordon Bennett, founder of *The New York Herald*, Baron Maurice Ephrussi de Rothschild and King George of Greece — who marvelled at this monument to the spirit of the ancients. Particularly praised were the mosaics, considered more luxurious than those in the finest fifth-century Athenian houses.

☿ **OPPOSITE & BELOW** Théodore Reinach decorated the villa with sculpture and mosaics which brought the aesthetics of the ancient world alive. Furniture, based on original Greek, Roman and Egyptian artifacts uncovered at archaeological digs or pictured in historical texts, was commissioned specially for each room. Exquisite stucco bas-reliefs were executed by sculptor Paul Jean-Baptiste Gascq.

☿ **OPPOSITE & BELOW** Owner Théodore Reinach's passion for ancient civilisation did not stop at the design and decoration of Villa Kérylos. He also lived the lifestyle. Each morning he dressed in a toga to visit his vast library — furnished with copies of Greek chairs, chaises and cabinets — where he would read, study and write. He ate and drank from Etruscan-style pottery and slept in a simple Greco-Roman-style bed.

☿ **LEFT & ABOVE** The courtyard within the villa was inspired by a Greek architectural device known as peristyle — essentially a colonnaded courtyard open to the sky, which allowed daily and seasonal changes in the sunlight to filter through to the living environment yet still offered cooling shade under its porticoes. According to ancient Greek tenets, the proportions of the courtyard are harmonious and symmetrical, retaining a human scale in order to create an intimate space.

☿ OPPOSITE & BELOW The site, a rocky outcrop which falls away to the sea, obliged the architect to structure an L-shaped villa rather than a square one. It incorporates balconies, terraces and pergolas staggered at different levels to make the most of the views out across the Mediterranean, and to catch the sun.

ITALIAN CHIC

› Portofino & the Italian Riviera ‹

Italian Chic

Just as the Côte d'Azur was establishing its own distinctive brand of glamour during the 1950s and 1960s, the neighbouring coastal charms of Italy were also being rediscovered and reinvented as a playground for the Italian nobility and home-grown cinema set. The eastern coast of Liguria had once attracted aristocrats from England and Russia to take health cures and spend the mild winters there. Writers and artists such as Lord Byron, Percy Bysshe Shelley, Marcel Proust, F. Scott Fitzgerald, D. H. Lawrence, Henry James, Claude Monet and Jean Cocteau had found its landscape, architecture and ambience inspirational.

The Italian Riviera, stretching south from Portofino to the coast of Rome, was rediscovered in the swinging sixties by a new set of admirers, both Italians and international jetsetters. After the grim years of World War Two, a new sense of hedonism infected those Italians with the money to seek solace in the simple and sensual pleasures of coastal life. It was, they decided, time to enjoy life again. But the escapism and "hard play" they sought was not in the ballrooms and grand villas of Venice or Florence as it might once have been. Rather it took the form of a pilgrimage to relaxed fishing villages with their unspoilt charm. In particular it focused on three distinctive resorts: Portofino, Forte dei Marmi and Porto Ercole.

These three coastal jewels became the favourite haunt of the aristocracy, of newly rich entrepreneurs, and of the burgeoning cinema scene in Rome, just a few hours drive away. The unique style of living they established in these places

OPPOSITE & RIGHT In the wake of European aristo-crats who had discovered the secluded beauty of resorts such as Portofino, Forte dei Marmi and Porto Ercole, movie stars and tycoons alike ventured there for discreet holidays. Elizabeth Taylor and Eddie Fisher in Portofino harbour; Aristotle Onassis on board the *Christina*.

came to symbolise Italy at its most glamorous. It was the Italy of bronzed and sultry beauties like Gina Lollobrigida, of tanned playboys in Riva speedboats, of a certain relaxed, carefree, even decadent attitude — a spirit that Fellini most famously dubbed "la dolce vita". This new mood was palpable in each of the three northern coastal resorts, yet each had its own special appeal.

Tucked away in a cove flanked by sheer cliffs, Portofino's dramatic setting and handsome architecture were the initial attraction for Italians looking to escape throughout the 1950s and 1960s. The tiny resort offered the character of a rustic fishing port, but it also had a rich cultural heritage and an air of refinement that especially appealed to European nobility. As was to be the case with many of the Riviera resorts, the social scene revolved around a particular hotel that became *the* place to be and be seen. In Portofino's case it was the Splendido. Perched high on a clifftop above the village, the Splendido was built in the local style, with sweeping terraces and lush gardens looking out over the Mediterranean. Its exclusivity made it a favourite haunt of the rich and celebrated, including the Duke of Windsor and Wallis Simpson. A long line of movie stars followed suit, establishing the hotel — along with Portofino itself — as the St Tropez of the Italian Riviera.

Further south, Forte dei Marmi became the favoured resort of the Tuscan nobility and of Rome's socialites and movie stars,

LEFT & OPPOSITE The press avidly followed in the footsteps of the aristocrats and celebrities who holidayed at the exclusive resorts fringing the coast between Genoa and Rome. Two much-photographed women were the Shah of Persia's wife, Empress Soraya — walking the cobbled streets of Portofino — and Sophia Loren — under the distinctive blue-and-white striped beach umbrellas of the Italian Riviera.

who flocked there for the long summer. The day revolved around the "bagni", or private beach clubs, that lined the long sandy beach. Each club claimed a separate strip, providing cabanas for changing, sun loungers and stripy beach umbrellas for reclining, as well as their own bars and clubs where the hedonistic pursuits continued long into the evening. Regardless of whether it was the America, the Bagno Rosina or the Bagno Piero that was the hot spot of the year, everyone would congregate at La Capannina for late-night partying. Marcello Mastroianni and actor-director Vittorio Gassman made Forte dei Marmi their summer stamping ground, and sealed the resort's reputation as hip and happening.

In contrast to the flat sands, sophisticated nightlife and openly hedonistic pursuits of Forte, Porto Ercole seemed remote and mystical. A seaside village on the Argentario Peninsula, a rugged promontory joined to the mainland by two thin bands of sand, Porto Ercole became the playground of the Roman aristocracy in the 1960s, when they deserted the more popular beaches near Rome in favour of this secluded spot. It mixed the graceful countryside and farmhouse architecture of Tuscany with a coastline of jagged cliffs and coves accessible only by boat. A sense of untamed nature gave it dramatic allure. In place of the extravagance found elsewhere on the Riviera, this unassuming resort was discreet and low-key — a mood epitomised by the Hotel Pellicano which, when it opened in 1965, sealed Porto Ercole's reputation as the most stylish of summer destinations.

♀ OPPOSITE & BELOW RIGHT Murals in the dining room of this elegant house on the Italian Riviera bring a sense of the outside indoors. They serve as an ever-present reminder of the ocean, and of the simple fishing boats that are such a characteristic component of the local seascape.

Coastal Sanctuary

O n the coast of Versilia, tucked away in a quiet village far from the tourist sights, an aristocratic Italian family have fused both a love of the sea and of antique Roman style in this sumptuous beachside villa. To do so they have radically reworked the original house that stood on the site, knocking down interior walls to create large, open living spaces — all oriented to make the most of the splendid coastal vistas.

Typical summer days unfold with mornings spent at the sandy beach across the street, then back home for a long lunch, perhaps followed by a siesta, with the hot afternoons whiled away in a garden that the owners refer to as their "little oasis". Reflecting their love of the outdoor lifestyle, they have made a very conscious attempt to bring the inside out and the outside in — integrating the mandates of living inside an enclosed dwelling with roof and walls, with its idyllic setting surrounded by sun, sea, sand and garden.

This approach is highly evident in the dining room with its vivid frescoes of outdoor scenes. The idea was to create the illusion of a room without walls, by transforming them into landscapes or seascapes which would give the impression of being in open space. Two of the walls are covered with murals of the countryside: one featuring mountainous terrain, the other, a seaside view, all executed in an evocative style redolent of the seventeenth century.

♀ OPPOSITE, LEFT & BELOW Most rooms open onto a long terrace that wraps around the villa. With its exposed beams, plain wicker chairs and rustic-style pillars, the terrace is as informal as the villa is grand. It provides a relaxed counterpoint to the more formal, Roman-inspired interiors, but still incorporates elegant details such as the shaped, shuttered doors with filigree brass handles.

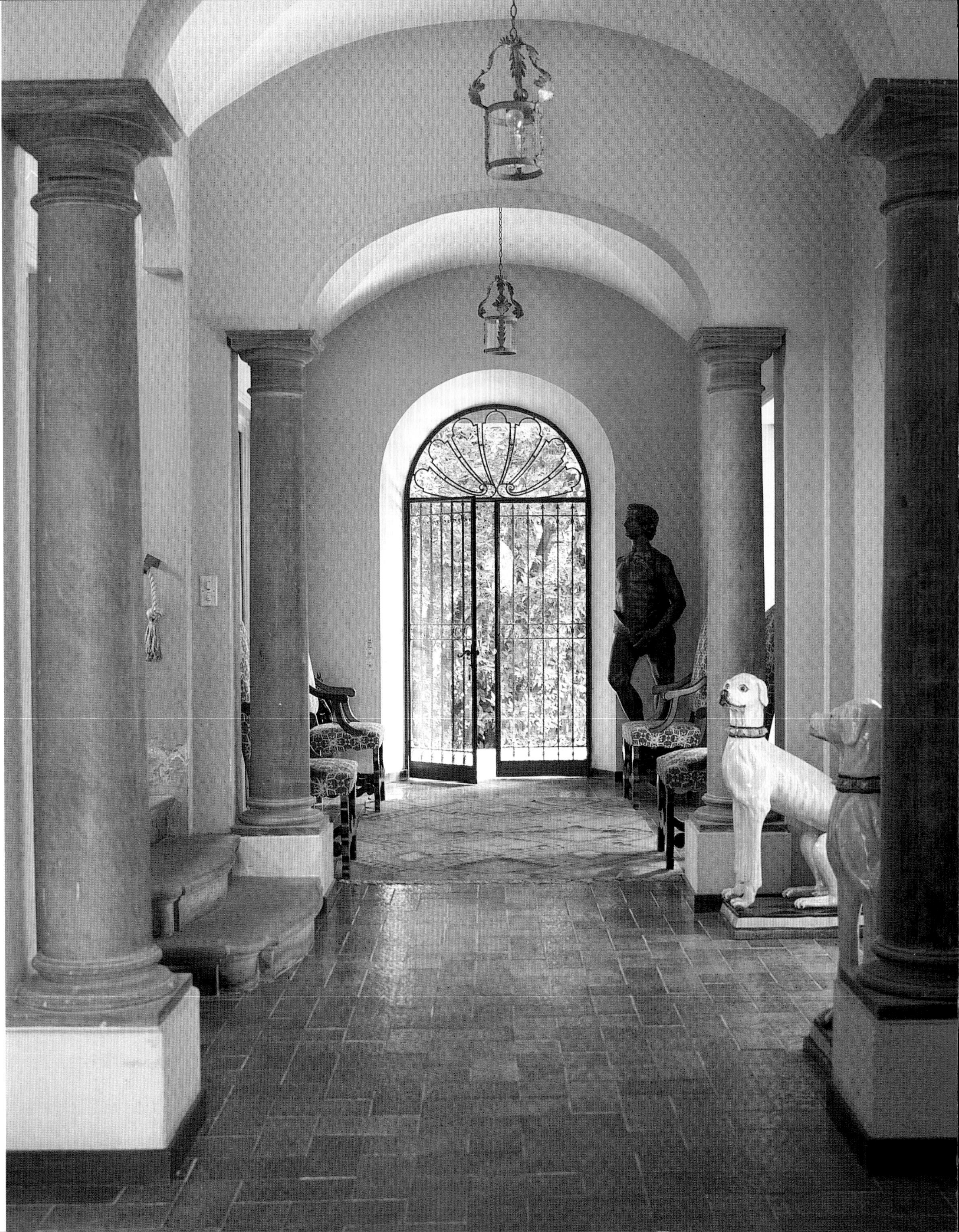

♀ OPPOSITE
& RIGHT

The grand entrance hall
and main living areas are
quintessentially Roman in
style. Interiors are marked
by graceful arches, floors
paved with burnished
terra-cotta tiles, Pepperino
columns and statuary.
The garden is filled with
fragrant laurel, a symbol
of the classical traditions
of the Roman Empire.

OPPOSITE & BELOW RIGHT The rugged cliffs and untamed landscape of Porto Ercole give Il Pellicano its sense of seclusion. The private beach with its rows of pristine sun loungers and parasols is accessible only by boat or a steep winding stairway.

Pleasure Principle

In its thirty-year anniversary issue, *L'Uomo Vogue* pondered the mystique of one of the Riviera's legendary hotels, conceived, like the magazine, in 1965: "I wonder what Il Pellicano would be today if it didn't owe its origins to a love affair! I wonder if it would indeed be the favourite hideaway of so many celebrities from all over the world …"

The hotel was in fact the product of a great love affair — between Englishman Michael Graham and Californian Patsy Daszel — and the story of their romance has become part of the Il Pellicano legend. The couple met after Michael, a well-known British adventurer and aviator, narrowly escaped death in an air crash in the African bush. Some time later he was posted to the United States under contract to Volkswagen and happened to attend a cocktail party to which Cole Porter had coaxed a reluctant Patsy. She had read about Michael in the papers and demanded to meet him. This chance encounter stirred love at first sight and eventually led to marriage.

Together the couple traversed Europe looking for a villa where they could settle down and run their own intimate hotel. They wanted the hotel to mirror the love and passion they felt for each other, to translate it into concrete form. After a long search, they stumbled upon a still unexplored stretch of the Monte Argentario, a jagged promontory that juts out into the Mediterranean from the Tuscan coast. They were instantly captivated and formed an immediate bond with the dramatic rocky

✷ RIGHT & OPPOSITE Il Pellicano's setting —
enclosed by pines and perched above the rugged cliffs
and dark blue waters of the Mediterranean — has
attracted admirers since ancient Roman times. The ruins
of luxurious Roman villas nearby attest to the eternal
appeal of the Argentario promontory.

landscape. The plot of land they purchased reminded them of Pelican Point in California where the romantic fireworks between them first began to spark and when, in 1965, they opened the hotel, they named it Il Pellicano.

Michael and Patsy wanted to recreate the mood of a country club rather than a hotel and to give the impression that guests were staying with friends. They built a main bungalow and several surrounding cottages, decorating each of the rooms in a different scheme. The combination of privacy and an air of casual chic resulted in an environment where guests would feel unhurried and perfectly relaxed. This sense of gracious ease was underpinned by the couple's innate charm, creating an irresistible magnet for style-conscious travellers in search of tranquillity. Throughout the latter half of the 1960s and beyond, it was *the* place for chic Romans to spend the summer. *Women's Wear Daily*, famed chronicler of the Beau Monde, was glowing in its praise: "… if you don't have your own villa, the only place to stay and still be 'in' is Il Pellicano." With its luxurious but simple style, dramatic setting and charismatic proprietors, as well as its proximity to Rome, Il Pellicano has remained firmly enscribed in the address books of the well-heeled and well-informed.

LEFT & BELOW For guests reluctant to venture down to the private beach, a serene saltwater swimming pool offers sea views and tranquil waters. It is set flush with a surround of local paving stones, creating the impression that the pool water and sea are one, separated only by a line of white umbrellas.

✺ **ABOVE & RIGHT** Rustic beams and whitewashed walls combine with plump sofas, elegant furnishings and scrolled flourishes on wrought-iron tables, mirrors and headboards to create an atmosphere of luxurious simplicity. The main sittting room is defined by a sculptural central fireplace, which becomes a focal point for socialising during the winter months. Throughout the hotel, enormous arched windows flood the interiors with bright Mediterranean light.

OPPOSITE & BELOW RIGHT The combination of centuries-old stone and a spell-binding view over the rugged coast of Porto Ercole creates a magical setting, reinforced by the fantastical imagery that runs through the interiors of this unusual home.

Celestial Sphere

Not surprisingly for the home of a jewellery designer, Elsa Peretti's base in Porto Ercole is purely sculptural. The villa is an ancient fortified tower, a work of art that seems to have been chiselled out of stone. With an interior by renowned Milanese architect and designer Renzo Mongiardino, the house gives the illusion of a ruin, but is luxuriously protected from the hazards of a real wreck exposed to the elements.

In Mongiardino's words: "A fascination with ruins inspired decorating schemes from the sixteenth century until the end of the nineteenth century. It was a very strong love for one's own past, but also for the present, in that ruins represent that which remained, that which could be observed tangibly in the landscape of one's own time."

This romantic view of ruins underpins the architect's idiosyncratic style, nowhere more so than in Elsa Peretti's home. Mongiardino took as his starting point the ruins of Clerisseau, which had deeply impressed him. He wanted to suggest a scenario of destruction, to invent rooms "of pure fantasy." In keeping with the look of a structure that has been ransacked, the extent of "destruction" varies from room to room. In the main living area, the ceiling appears to have collapsed in one corner, offering a view of the sky above, while in an intimate sitting room on the lower level of the tower, the sense of decay is more extreme. The images Mongiardino painted on the walls and ceiling not only depict an evocative ruined state, they also serve

The monumental architecture of the medieval stone tower is dramatically set off by the lush landscape, including a garden planted with hardy coastal varieties and vivid flowering shrubs. A simple wooden table and benches on the terrace are in perfect harmony with their rugged surroundings.

to visually enlarge the space itself. With their apparently crumbling masonry and clinging vines, the walls give the illusion that outside and inside are merging, creating a sense of openness in what might have been an otherwise claustrophobic room.

The beamed ceiling likewise gives the impression that the room is disintegrating. The roof appears to be in a state of collapse, offering glimpses of the sky above, while vines take hold of what remains. Dominating this other-worldly scene is a large stucco fireplace, inspired by the carved monsters in the famed garden of Bomarzo. In contrast to the flat, highly decorated wall and ceiling surfaces, the hearth is a solid three-dimensional presence and seems to leap from the wall, energising the motionless world of the ruin.

Within Mongiardino's imposing faux-architectural setting, simple furnishings have been used to create the mood of contemporary rustic living. As befits the home of a modern jewellery designer, everything from paint to furnishings has a sculptural feel, as though molten silver has been poured in and left to take shape. The whole interior environment is at once romantic, mysterious, voluptuous and magical — steeped in history and the elements of form.

OPPOSITE Interior designer Mongiardino is a master of special paint effects as well as a passionate afficionado of romantic ruins. To capture the spirit of the once-abandoned tower, he created trompe l'oeil coffers on the ceiling, with sections open to an illusory sky.

RIGHT High in the tower, a small window offers spectacular views of the ocean from this charming guest bedroom. Wooden beds, an antique washstand and delicate floral wallcovering conjure up an old-world atmosphere. The room's soft, feminine quality is in stark contrast to the raw stone exterior and wild terrain.

ABOVE In one of the narrow stairwells that connects each level of the tower, a rustic sculpture sits atop an antique capital, speaking volumes about jewellery designer Elsa Peretti's rapport with the sensuality of form. It also reflects the interior mix of earthy and ornate decorative elements.

LEFT & BELOW A downstairs sitting room is dominated by a dramatic carved stone fireplace, evocative of ancient Rome as well as the Renaissance. The use of clever painted effects — for faux columns, architectural details, even a wooden door, all in an apparent state of deterioration — creates a room setting which is pure theatre.

⟨ OPPOSITE & BELOW RIGHT To the owners of this Portofino villa, the combination of crisp white tones and traditional English chintzes spells the ultimate in chic. Everything in the home is carefully chosen and arranged — including collections of old-fashioned model ships and country pottery — but the effect is one of relaxed charm.

Pristine Scheme

Born in Genoa, Pupi Fattori has always had a love for her native region with its painted facades and spectacular views of the sapphire-blue sea. Despite these strong local ties, Pupi's name is in fact synonymous with Milan, where she is something of a fashion doyenne. She likes to think of herself as a purveyor of "classically chic" clothing for men, women and children, and her philosophy of outfitting people is much like her vision for furnishing houses — a complete lifestyle approach. With a razor-sharp eye she carefully selects individual elements, which are not necessarily matched, then assembles them to create a total look.

Her choice of Portofino as a place to get away from it all, as well as her choice of a house and interior scheme, are very much a reflection of her personal style. When she first found the Portofino house in 1984, she was struck by the charms of a ruin desperately in need of tender loving care, and by the spellbinding views from its lofty mountain setting. She purchased it together with then-husband Giorgio Host-Ivessich, an architect, who immediately turned his talents to designing and converting the interior spaces. Pupi, meanwhile, took charge of the decoration, which she wanted to be "feminine and country" but also "dressed", as she would her clients, with a melange of her favourite things.

The sense of interior airiness and openness was achieved principally through the expanses of whitewashed wall that

LEFT Gauzy white curtains, hung from a slender wrought-iron bar, float in the cooling breeze that blows in from Portofino harbour. The airy sitting room embodies the owners' love of peaceful village life and of eclectic English country style. Freshly cut flowers from the garden are in evidence everywhere.

characterise each room. To Pupi, white is the essence of Portofino. As she sees it, white is also the essence of country style, an essentially relaxing tone that reminds her of the places she adores, such as Venice, Paris and Milan. White also makes an ideal backdrop for showing off her other stylistic passions. She loves English chintz, so much of the fabric used for sofas, armchairs, curtains and bedding was sourced at Colefax & Fowler. Pottery is another obsession and collections of Art Deco and Majolica ceramics are clustered together on shelves and side tables throughout the house. Some of the pieces were bought in London and carted home; some were found in Milan and others locally.

Pupi divides her time between a flat in Milan, where she runs her thriving fashion business and boutique, and her Portofino retreat, which she shares with her husband Giorgio Fattori. The couple love to spend time together in their hideaway: the silence, the absence of cars and the glimpses of water all around combine to give them an enormous sense of peace. Pupi finds few greater pleasures than flopping in an easy chair on the veranda and immersing herself in a favourite book, occasionally raising her eyes to take in vistas of the old port and the sparkling Bay of Portofino.

BELOW & RIGHT Owner Pupi Fattori is a self-confessed bower bird, who loves to comb flea markets in both her native Italy and in England in search of porcelain, pottery, silverware and other decorative objects. Displays of favourite objects join framed prints and niches lined with books in adding character to the living room, while pretty antique crockery pieces are used to set the dining table.

☾ **LEFT** Echoing the use of English chintzes elsewhere in the house, the bedroom is decorated with traditional English country prints. Bedlinen scattered with sprigs of violets and piles of lacy pillows create a feminine retreat.

BELOW & OPPOSITE Lengths of handmade cotton lace are used to form sheer curtains in the bathroom, beautifully filtering the light and adding an undeniably romantic touch.

Portofino Jewel

The legendary Hotel Splendido is, as its name suggests, sublime, its setting and atmosphere arguably among the most rarefied of the Italian Riviera. Perched on a cliff overlooking the fishing village of Portofino, the Splendido has commanded the tiny port for more than a century, providing a luxurious refuge for those disposed to travelling in high style. But the clifftop location has not always attracted such elegant visitors. It was originally the site of a Benedictine monastery, which was ransacked by Saracen pirates so frequently that the monks fled, leaving the building to fall into decay, its ruins inhabited only by stray sheep. In the nineteenth century, an Italian aristocrat, Baron Baratta, rebuilt the ruined structure to create a grand summer villa. It was transformed into a hotel in 1901 by Ruggero Valentini, a pioneer of tourism to Portofino.

Built in the local style, with airy interior spaces and a painted facade covered in vines, the Splendido's real charm lies in its extraordinary environment. It is set in four acres of exotic gardens, the lush foliage shrouding the hotel buildings and spilling down to the edge of the cliff face. Candlelit dinners on the hotel terrace provide intoxicating views of the twinkling port below and the sea beyond, framed by a bower of flowering bougainvillea. Exotic plants were considered de rigueur for coastal landscaping when the hotel was built, and the terraced beds of the garden are now studded with towering palms, yew,

LEFT & OPPOSITE Few views along the Italian Riviera can rival that of the Splendido. Perched on the pine-covered hillside above the famed yacht harbour of Portofino, the hotel is built long and low to make the most of the panoramic outlook.

sea pines and mimosa. Silvery olive groves and wild herbs glisten in the sun by day and exude a heady fragrance at night. Narrow paths wind through the gardens and along the clifftop, twisting down to the sleepy village of Portofino.

In the heart of the port stands the Splendido's more recently constructed sister, the Splendido Mare. With its peach-tinted facade, sunny yellow window frames and green shutters, it is the jewel in the crown of the tiny village piazza, enclosed by a medley of trompe l'oeil-painted facades. Opposite lies the rippling water of the port, bobbing with yachts and painted dinghies and lined with clusters of outdoor cafés, bars and restaurants.

The ambience of this quaint fishing village and the spellbinding coastal views it affords, have attracted a string of well-heeled visitors to the Splendido over the years. The guest book contains names of the noble, the celebrated and the jet set who have passed through the hotel doors. The Duke of Windsor and Wallis Simpson were the first to put their pens to paper here in 1952. Then followed Lauren Bacall, Humphrey Bogart, Elizabeth Taylor, Richard Burton, Clark Gable and Ava Gardner, Catherine Deneuve, Liza Minnelli and Rex Harrison. Harrison was so enchanted with the spot that he eventually purchased his own villa nearby. He became a magnet for the film crowd, who played out their own version of *La Dolce Vita* in local bars and restaurants and on the terrace of the Splendido.

 **ABOVE & RIGHT** The quintessential Riviera scene: yachts moored in the sparkling blue-green Mediterranean and an elegant swimming pool sited high above, surrounded by neat rows of loungers and crisp white sun umbrellas. For those who want to venture beyond this secluded spot, the Splendido's private speedboat lies ready to whisk guests to nearby Santa Margherita beach or the golf course at Rapallo.

☺ ABOVE, LEFT & RIGHT Each room in the hotel is decorated individually in modern Mediterranean style. Defining features include polished timber floors and a palette of soft, soothing colours. Nothing jars the eye or distracts from the view.

RIGHT The architecture of the hotel, once a nineteenth-century villa, is typical of Portofino in its use of jewel-like exterior colours, painted shutters and a profusion of clinging vines. The rhythm of the sensuously curving balcony partitions conjures up images of the gentle roll of waves in the harbour below.

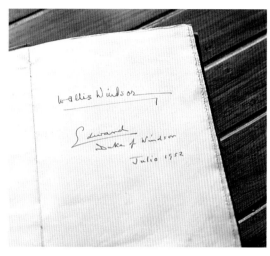

OPPOSITE With its tiled chequerboard floor, graceful arches and dusky colour scheme, the hotel lobbycreates the mood of an intimate Italian palazzo. Lining the walls are photographs of famous guests.

LEFT The Splendido's long list of celebrity guests has made it a landmark on the Italian Riviera, and undoubtedly adds to its contemporary appeal. Among those that have left a reminder of their stay are the Duke of Windsor and Wallis Simpson; Princess Margarethe of Sweden; ballerina Norma Shearer; and actress Maggie Smith.

BAREFOOT CHARM

› Capri & the Amalfi Coast ‹

OPPOSITE No dress code was required for holidays on the Amalfi Coast. Even the immaculate Jacqueline Kennedy looked perfectly at home there in swimsuit and bare feet, as did daughter Caroline and her playmate.

Barefoot Charm

If the image of a young bikini-clad Brigitte Bardot has come to encapsulate the glamour of St Tropez and the Côte d'Azur in its heyday, then it is the vision of a tanned, barefoot Sophia Loren that most vividly captures the appeal of Capri and the Amalfi Coast. Extrovert, tempestuous, voluptuous, capricious, the young Loren seemed to symbolise the wild scenery, carefree atmosphere and earthy, sensual style of living that make the coastline and islands off Naples so bewitching.

It is certain that appearing in films such as *It Started in Naples,* set in and around her home town, went some way to making Loren synonymous with the beauty of southern Italy's coast. And when cinema audiences in Rome, New York or London saw her diving from rocks into clear Mediterranean water, sunning herself on the timber deck of a fishing boat, flirting with bronzed young Adonises or gazing at the horizon from high on an island clifftop, it set a fashion for the Amalfi Coast and Capri that lasted throughout the 1950s and beyond.

On the Amalfi Coast, Positano was the most popular of the mainland resorts — a tiny fishing village nestled in a rocky cove. Here, hotels like the Sirenuse or San Pietro, perched dramatically on sheer cliffs, offered a taste of laid-back luxury against one of the world's most inspirational landscapes. Capri, meanwhile, had the aura of an enchanted island. It was a ready-made movie set, the perfect backdrop for steamy romances and tempestuous dramas with its rugged limestone cliffs, underwater caves and grottoes, transparent blue water, views across the sea to Naples and Mount Vesuvius, lush woods of evergreens and the

OPPOSITE & LEFT The Duke of Windsor and Wallis Simpson were frequent visitors to the coast of Italy, attracted by the sun, dazzling seascapes and charming village atmosphere of harbour towns like Positano.

old town of Capri itself. Indeed, something of the island's mystique is owed to a history dating back to ancient Greek times. Legend has it that Grecians from the Ionian Sea settled on Capri during the eighth century BC, and parts of an ancient acropolis attest to their likely presence. There are other traces of Greek civilisation on the island up to the sixth and seventh centuries, when the inhabitants settled by the sea and built terraced houses to face the sun and water. This Greek heritage was one of the attractions for Octavianus Caesar, later Emperor Augustus, who chose Capri as his summer residence. It offered peace, good weather and the exoticism of the Greek presence. He loved to hold feasts and parties on balmy starlit evenings and encouraged the local Greeks and Romans to swap clothes and speak in each other's language.

These idyllic days were a foretaste of the delights Capri offered up to its twentieth-century invaders, but the intervening years saw the island the subject of a power struggle during which it passed from Roman Imperial hands to those of numerous European duchies and kingdoms that laid claim to its charms, and to its strategic position. In the nineteenth century, the classical history, unrivalled setting and rustic way of life appealed to the Romantics of northern Europe. It was an essential stop on the Grand Tours of the wealthy who travelled south in search of gentle pleasures and intellectual enlightenment.

But it was only really in the 1950s, when moviemakers discovered Capri as a natural location for their films, that it acquired a new cachet. Its raw energy, clarity of light and the blue of its water made it a picture postcard backdrop for the

LEFT & ABOVE Clark Gable and native Neapolitan Sophia Loren brought the charms of Capri to the silver screen in the 1960 film *It Started in Naples*. Hollywood exposure generated a huge fascination for the tiny island with its quaint harbour and dazzling setting. As always, Loren's presence attracted the attentions of local admirers.

OPPOSITE & RIGHT A mixture of breathtaking coastal scenery and a casual approach to living made Capri and the Amalfi Coast hugely appealing. It fuelled dreams of escaping to the characteristic fishing villages with their simple way of life, seemingly endless days of Mediterranean sunshine and tanned, lithe inhabitants. Playboys like Dado Ruspoli, pictured right, embodied the hedonistic Riviera attitude.

glamorous stars of the day. As its reputation spread it attracted not only movie stars from Rome; Hollywood too became entranced by this seductive corner of Italy, as did royalty and high society. Rita Hayworth was one of the first to arrive on the scene, causing a sensation when she sailed into Capri with her husband Ali Khan on board Errol Flynn's yacht. Stepping out on deck looking suntanned, hair tousled by the wind, and wearing a simple strapless cotton dress and flat navy shoes, she set a trend for vacationing in Capri, and for a fresh, relaxed way of dressing. Even today it is not hard to imagine Sophia Loren, Elizabeth Taylor or Jackie O alighting from private yachts in tiny Capri harbour, clad in the distinctive slender cropped trousers and sleeveless shirts made by local designers, their feet shod in the whimsical flat sandals hand-crafted by the shoemakers of nearby Positano.

This is all part of the dream that is the Amalfi Coast. Whether taking in the splendid views of perched Positano with its tiny port, winding streets and painted facades, or snaking along Capri's hilly pedestrian paths, brimming with fragrant blossoms and dotted with chic boutiques and restaurants, the experience is seductively irresistible. The natural setting, ancient history, placid fishing villages and carefree spirit of Capri and the Amalfi Coast have made them a mecca for film stars and the jet set, a place where it is impossible not to live "la dolce vita".

OPPOSITE & BELOW RIGHT The spectacular setting of Dino Trappetti's house, on a Capri clifftop with panoramic views, dictates that life is lived primarily on the terrace, which catches the sun from dawn till dusk. It is only in the winter months that living moves back indoors.

Cinematic View

The tale of Dino Trappetti's villa, Il Canile, in Capri, unfolds like a movie script. Nothing could be more fitting for the owner of Costumi Tirelli in Rome, which has created costumes for some of the world's best-known theatre productions and films, from classics of the Italian cinema by Visconti and Fellini to modern masterpieces like *The Age of Innocence*, *The English Patient* and *Titanic*.

Trappetti's villa was once, unbelievably, the "canile", or kennels, for the dogs of Comte Vismara, who lived in a grand house on the same property. The estate was later owned by Norma Clark, an American of Swedish descent, who eventually sold up. The main villa became the Hotel Punta Tragara, while the kennel was sold to Trappetti and three of his closest friends: cinema couturier Umberto Tirelli; actress Lucia Bose, who had just divorced her husband, the famous Spanish toreador Luis-Miguel Dominguin; and Isa de Simone. Eventually the two women sold their shares to the two men, but on Tirelli's death Trappetti inherited the cherished home along with the costume business in Rome.

The director of Costumi Tirelli now spends his summers at the bijou villa and has decorated it to reflect the elemental living style that is the essence of Capri. Blue and white dominate the interior scheme, echoing the crisp whitewashed facades of the island houses and the deep azure of the Mediterranean.

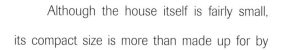 RIGHT Throughout the summer the house is filled with friends from Rome and the terrace becomes the natural centre of attention. Outdoor settings dot the length of the multi-level terrace, providing ample space for sunbathing and snoozing.

OPPOSITE Framed by a border of deep green foliage, the rustic dining room is completely open to the terrace — a magical setting for candlelit evening meals.

Although the house itself is fairly small, its compact size is more than made up for by a huge deck with views of the sea. For Trappetti, its landscaped terraces, spilling over with colourful flowering shrubs and exotic trees, form the most charming visual aspect of the home and are a favourite spot for relaxing. The lush greenery is kept in pristine condition by a talented gardener, known to the locals simply as Costanzo.

Il Canile is clearly Trappetti's haven from business matters in Rome and also the hub of a busy social life. Throughout the summer months, the terrace is alive with friends from the fashion and art worlds, who dot its dazzling white backdrop like actors on the set of a Fellini film.

Despite his regular mid-year escape to Capri, Trappetti is passionate about costume, taking an active role in fashioning actors and actresses to fit their parts. His current preoccupation is the Tirelli Collection in Rome, a new museum within an eighteenth-century house. The museum will be dedicated not only to the art of the costumier, but also to the creative genius behind Italy's renowned costume house, Umberto Tirelli.

BELOW & RIGHT The terrace is a natural suntrap, providing an ideal environment for plantings of Mediterranean trees and flowering plants to flourish. This lush, leafy terrace is much-cherished and demands the regular attentions of a local gardener. Inside, the obsession with greenery continues, with potted plants and vines blurring the boundary between interior spaces and the terrace outside.

 ABOVE & OPPOSITE Inside, blue and white is the dominant theme. This colour
scheme is symbolic of Capri — representing the union of the traditional whitewashed
island houses and the surrounding sea. The fireplace, reserved for cool winter evenings,
is surrounded by the owner's collection of dog statuettes. They serve as a reminder of
the history of the house, which was formerly a kennel.

🦀 **OPPOSITE & BELOW RIGHT** A postcard view of the jagged Faraglioni rocks jutting from the sea, and a terrace garden of olive trees, native lemon trees and fragrant flowers attest to the irresistible appeal of life on the island of Capri.

Ivory Tower

The owners of this villa were looking for the best of all possible worlds when they began their search for a bolthole that would offer an alternative to their base in Tuscany. They wanted peace and quiet, an inspiring setting, proximity to both a lively social scene and places of cultural interest, and easy access to the aquatic pursuits for which the Amalfi Coast is justly famous. Their brief was satisfied by an unspoilt corner on the island of Capri.

The couple fell in love with Capri's informal yet chic atmosphere and, not surprisingly, its position and brilliant views. They were beguiled not only by its physical beauty, but also by its proximity to the fascinations of the mainland, just a boat ride away. For jet-set village life or even city lights, they could take the ferry to Amalfi. And for intellectual stimulation, they could visit nearby Pompeii to delight in the painted decoration of the villas there, which reveal ancient Roman civilisation at its most sophisticated.

As a base for their excursions and adventures, the couple settled on a small house, just big enough to comfortably accommodate them but not so big as to demand time-consuming upkeep. They bought the house from a writer who had constructed it in 1964 as his retreat, and it matched their needs so perfectly that they have changed very little about it. Nevertheless they have made the picturesque villa very much their own, decorating it with an artful eye that mixes

OPPOSITE & LEFT The secluded swimming pool appears to have been carved out of the sheer cliff face. To harmonise with the leafy setting and sea beyond, the pool was lined with a coat of grey emulsion, which gives the water its rich turquoise appearance. Matching turquoise sun loungers complete this idyllic scene.

classical antiques with ethnic rugs, textiles and simple earthy furnishings, all set against bright whitewashed walls. Vivid splashes of red, calming sage green, radiant blue and sunny yellow bring a sense of warmth and emotional wellbeing to the relaxed interiors. The overall mood is one of tranquillity and peace, the perfect place for reviving flagging spirits.

The focal point of this island hideaway is the terrace, divided into several separate living areas: a sweet vine-covered balcony for breakfast caffé latté; a dining alcove furnished with scrubbed wooden table and wicker chairs; a secluded swimming pool; and a sweeping stretch of terra-cotta-paved patio, set with outdoor sofa and sunloungers. All this overlooks a stunning coastal panorama taking in the port and township of Capri, a vast unbroken swathe of Mediterranean blue and, as the focal point, the Faraglioni — two enormous volcanic rocks jutting out of the sea that are symbolic of Capri itself. Whether sitting on the terrace in summer or whiling away the hours in the drawing room during winter, the owners of this villa never cease to delight in the view of the Faraglioni — an ever-present reminder of what drew them here in the first place.

OPPOSITE & BELOW The steep site is arranged over several terraced levels, each with its own pergola or outdoor furniture. On the main terrace, a rustic reed-covered trellis provides shade during the long hot summer days. Lunch is served at a big wooden farmhouse table surrounded by wicker chairs.

🦀 OPPOSITE & ABOVE A bare whitewashed backdrop — typical of houses on Capri — is enlivened with bold splashes of zinging colour, richly decorated textiles and objects collected on the couple's frequent trips abroad. A section of cliff, from which the house was hewn, provides a feature wall in the bedroom, its rough surface offset by piles of luxurious tasselled pillows. In the dining room, a pedestal table is paired with Italian Empire chairs and a white chaise longue studded with gem-like cushions, while in the lounge room (overleaf), low-level seating, ethnic rugs, stacked baskets and piles of books create a more relaxed mood.

Sheer Indulgence

The Hotel San Pietro is an architectural tour de force that capitalises on one of the most spellbinding settings in the world: the dramatic Amalfi coastline with its craggy cliffs rising out of the sea like majestic mountains, seeming more like the chef d'oeuvre of a surrealist sculptor's chisel than the result of natural forces. It was the overwhelming potential of this unspoilt backdrop that so captivated Carlo Cinque, who envisioned it as the perfect setting for an intimate and luxurious hotel that would boast the ultimate "rooms with a view".

Raised as the son of a hotelier in the delightful village of nearby Positano, Cinque's charm and unbounding enthusiasm made him the perfect candidate for creating an albergo of his own. In 1962, as the first step to realising that dream, he purchased a peak of rocky cliff face, barren except for the tiny ancient chapel of San Pietro. The site was accessed via hair-raising roads from Positano and the only neighbours were jagged promontories and the blanket of blue sea which lay below.

Cinque began to build himself a villa, not perched on top of the cliff but actually carved into it — no mean feat. Miraculously, he succeeded in creating a small apartment and even a garden, without which no Italian coastal home would be complete. He continued to carve into the cliff face crafting additional rooms one by one, and after eight years of what must have been back-breaking hard labour, he had constructed

RIGHT & OPPOSITE The design of the hotel is intended to perfectly reflect the natural lines of the rocky coast. It was painstakingly carved from one of the most impressive spurs on the Amalfi Coast, and is famous for its terraces lined with brilliant yellow banquettes, each decorated with locally made ceramic tiles.

a hotel with thirty-three rooms facing the sea, as well as a wide terrace, so divinely situated that al fresco diners found themselves tempted to dive off into the translucent water below.

The San Pietro has since expanded to sixty rooms, each tucked away into a series of ledges to ensure maximum privacy and tranquillity. Fragrant regional flowers colourfully drape and spill from trellised balconies and trickle down the hilly landscape to the private beach below. Vines and grape arbours sprawl across porches to provide shade from the brilliant sunshine. Benches on outdoor terraces are covered with ceramic tiles, which together with ceramic plaques and trompe l'oeil paint effects, evoke the decorative spirit of nearby Pompeii with its fanciful frescoed Roman motifs. They also evoke the spirit of Amalfi's local potters, who produce colourful handmade ceramics in whimsical shapes.

In spite of a guest list that has included Catherine Deneuve, Gore Vidal and Franco Zeffirelli, the San Pietro has remained a family affair, run since Carlo Cinque's death by his nephew and niece Salvatore and Virginia Alfanasio. Appropriately they have retained the original hotel name, taken from the ancient chapel that greets guests as they arrive. They have also remained true to Cinque's grand vision of a luxurious environment at one with its rugged setting.

BELOW & OPPOSITE The interior of the lounge area looks more like that of an exquisite private villa than a hotel. The overall effect is one of great refinement and taste, with curvaceous whitewashed forms and terra-cotta floors serving as a rusticated backdrop to restrained yet luxurious furnishings and exceptional details such as the wrought-iron balustrade and swirling floor inset of handmade ceramic tiles.

Private Paradise

On a tiny group of private islands off the coast from Positano sits one of the most unusual homes on the Riviera. It is special not only for its splendid physical setting, on one of three jagged rocks rising from the sea, but also for its history. The story of Li Galli, as this tiny archipelago is called, dates back to mythical times, when the Greeks nicknamed it Le Sirenuse, the home of the sirens. Despite the reputation of these beguiling creatures who would lure sailors to their deaths, the dramatic islands of Li Galli have proved compelling to centuries of intrepid seafarers.

In the days of the Emperor Tiberius, a Roman villa was built on Li Galli, perhaps for the emperor himself who is reputed to have sailed there with his court in the hopes of hearing the sirens singing. Traces of this first inhabitance on the islands remain, as does a medieval tower built by the Saracens in the eleventh century. They, like others since, prized Li Galli for its strategic significance. However, it is the most recent residents on the island who have stamped it with their own character to bring this ancient site to life.

The Russian-born choreographer Léonide Massine was responsible for changing the essential nature of the Li Galli archipelago from a place of defence and fortification to a private hideaway. Massine bought the islands in the 1920s, when

they had ceased to be of use to anyone strategically, and eventually set about constructing a villa on the site of the original Roman structure. To design the house, he commissioned his friend Le Corbusier, who made the most of the expansive views in his plan. Le Corbusier situated a large terrace garden on the first floor, facing Capri and Cape Licosa, and located the bedrooms on the other side of the villa, facing Positano and the Lattari Mountains.

Once the villa was completed, Li Galli became a creative base for Massine. He restored the old watchtower to use as a dance studio and alternative residence, installing a large dance floor, a mezzanine that could hold a quartet, and an open-air theatre, since destroyed in a storm. Even after his death in 1979, Massine's passion for dance continued to be played out on the islands, when they became a retreat for Rudolf Nureyev. The ballet dancer indulged his passion for the Islamic world, redecorating the villa in the Moorish style and cladding its interiors with specially commissioned tiles. However, the islands served as Nureyev's exotic citadel for just a few years until his death.

By the time Li Galli was bought by its new and current owner, hotelier Giovanni Russo, much had fallen into disrepair. Now restoring it back to life has become Russo's passion. When he is not running his two hotels in Sorrento, he spends time at Li Galli overseeing work on the buildings and grounds. Summers are spent enjoying the beauty of the islands' unmatched setting, with friends always welcome to share a piece of this private paradise.

OPPOSITE Present owner Giovanni Russo lives in a Saracen watchtower that dates from the eleventh century, while the two houses on the island provide private quarters for visiting friends.

LEFT Both terrace and fountain were built by Léonide Massine when he lived at Li Galli. The choreographer used the terrace as a stage for dance practice and private performances, but it now serves as the setting for more conventional entertaining. A pair of ornate stone chairs, copies of ancient Roman designs, provide suitably theatrical seating for contemplating the horizon.

OPPOSITE & LEFT
The bedrooms in the
island's main villa are
largely still as Nureyev
left them, although much
of the furniture was sold
at auction. Despite living
here for only a few
years, Nureyev left an
indelible mark on the
villa, with his vision for
a Moorish-style retreat
where dancers and
choreographers could
come for inspiration.

O **OPPOSITE & BELOW RIGHT** The Villa San Michele has become a Capri landmark. Once the home of scientist, philosopher and scholar Axel Munthe, the splendid villa is now a museum dedicated to its former owner's ideas. On the terrace, a stone sphinx looks out to sea, a symbol of Munthe's passion for antiquity and archaeology.

Breathing Space

igh on a cliff in Anacapri stands the Villa San Michele, where Swedish scientist, scholar, author and philanthropist, Axel Munthe, lived and worked. He began to build this exceptional villa in 1896 after falling in love with the spot during a trip to Naples. In his book, *The History of St Michael*, published in 1940, he vividly described his first encounter with the site, reached after a long climb to a rocky plateau: "The whole Gulf of Naples was at our feet, surrounded by Ischia, Procida, Posillipo, decorated by pines, the scintillating white line of Naples, Vesuvius with its pinkish cloud of smoke, the plains of Sorrento protected by Monte Sant' Angelo and the faraway Apennines covered in snow."

Confronted by this astonishing outlook, Munthe needed little convincing that here was the perfect place to build a house: a place for contemplation, for rest and writing. Inspiring the construction of the villa were the ruins of a small chapel on the site. The vaulted ceiling of the chapel had long since collapsed, leaving large vertical blocks of stone rising out of the rubble of collapsed walls. Its ancient spirit was the catalyst for the house, which was named, like the chapel, after Saint Michael. The villa was built over a space of five years. Although small in size, with only a handful of rooms, it is the surrounding terraces that lend Villa San Michele its essential character. As Munthe himself described it, there were "… the loggias, the terraces and

♂ RIGHT & OPPOSITE Both the architecture of the villa and its outlook embody the quintessential Capri. With its plain, whitewashed facade, use of columns, arrangement around an inner courtyard and orientation to the sea, Villa San Michele is characteristic of the style made popular when the Romans colonised the island.

the bowers all around the villa, where one could look at the sun, the sea, and the clouds — the soul needs more room to breathe than the body."

Architecturally the villa incorporates a harmonious mix of local historical styles. Capri was originally colonised by the ancient Romans and much of the island is still dotted with vestiges of ancient Roman architecture. Then, like other dreamy Riviera settings, it experienced the building boom of the late nineteenth century, evolving its own regional version of the belle époque — a style dubbed "Capreses". It referred to the rustic, white-washed villas, oriented to the sea and the sky, that became the norm in Capri, in stark contrast to the highly ornamental approach associated with the French Riviera. The Villa San Michele incorporates both Roman and Capreses influences, with a beautiful, well-proportioned exterior, arched loggias, vaulted ceilings and classical columns derived from ancient architecture. Mosaic floors, antique sculptures and busts complete the interior scheme. Gardens, terraces and arbours blossom with flowers, paying tribute to the natural flora, as well as the nineteenth-century taste for exotic plants.

It was Axel Munthe's wish that the house he so treasured should become a museum after his death. Fittingly, his former home also plays host to visiting scholars and humanists, who can immerse themselves in the atmosphere that inspired the great visionary, studying not only his philosophies and scientific legacy, but also his finely honed sense of aesthetics.

ↀ OPPOSITE & LEFT

The villa has been kept
much as Axel Munthe
left it. Manifestations of
antiquity are everywhere,
whether in the form of
a Grecian-style sculpture
flanked by marble
columns, a sculpted mask
encircled by vines or a
mosaic floor inlaid with
aquatic motifs.

♂ RIGHT The strong architectural lines of the interior are relieved in this drawing room by an injection of soft colour and decorative pattern. Italian furniture, painted in shades of gold and blue, echoes the mosaic floor.

BELOW A simple and functional kitchen in pristine white is dominated by a monumental tiled unit that serves as work surface, stove top, sink and oven. Original copper pans line the walls and hang from the ceiling.

Ò LEFT A loggia is a quintessential feature of an Italian coastal villa, a physical manifestation of the ancient Greek and Roman rapport with sky, sun and sea, and of their attempt to create an architecture that would harmonise interior and exterior elements — in both public buildings and private villas.

Ò OPPOSITE At Villa San Michele, the loggia serves as a gallery showcasing Axel Munthe's vast collection of antique sculpture and artifacts. Busts mounted on columns and pedestals line the long corridor, while architectural fragments, sculptures and antique furniture jostle for space. All are reminders of Munthe's obsession with antiquity.

★ OPPOSITE The bougainvillea-draped terrace is the Sersales' favourite part of the flat. Large glass doors connect it to the lounge and dining rooms, making it an extension of the living areas and allowing sunlight and harbour breezes to filter through.

Positano Spirit

When Antonio and Carla Sersale inherited the direction of the renowned Le Sirenuse Hotel in Positano, they lived there for two years while looking for a more intimate base to call home. However, when your family's former country house-cum-hotel is one of the grandest buildings in Positano, boasting a perfect view, everything else seems second best. Eventually though, the couple found just what they wanted: a secluded two-level flat in a 200-year-old UNESCO-listed building, its facade virtually hidden from the hilly street entrance but offering broad glimpses of the sea.

In keeping with the historic significance of their new home, the Sersales created an interior with plenty of authentic local charm. The whitewashed walls and plain tiled floors evoke the natural simplicity of a village house, while providing a backdrop to textiles and furnishings gathered on the couple's travels. Antonio boasts an array of Oriental textiles, carpets, weavings and needlework, bought when he lived for a time in Persia. Now the collection includes Indian, Chinese and Turkish pieces as well, which provide striking splashes of colour and texture against the bright white walls. On the terrace, very little in the way of decoration has been required. Here it is the elements of nature that provide the visual interest. Pink bougainvillea drapes itself over the walls, while the photographic coastal views capture the essence of what life in Positano is all about.

✷ **LEFT & BELOW** A strong Eastern flavour permeates the interiors, but without compromising their essentially relaxed and rustic flavour. A traditional Positano stucco niche melds beautifully with safari chairs, Orientalist textile borders and a Moroccan-style light. A terra-cotta floor and potted palms give the feel of the outdoors.

✳ BELOW, RIGHT & OPPOSITE When their busy schedule managing the
Sirenuse Hotel allows the couple time off, they indulge their passion for travel to Asia
and the Middle East. Exquisite textiles collected en route add luxurious texture and rich
colour to the simple white interior spaces with their high ceilings and arched doorways.

♆ **OPPOSITE & BELOW RIGHT** Perched above a sheer cliff facing the Gulf of Naples, Villa Tritone and its extraordinary garden are protected from the elements by a stone wall inset with Triforium arches, through which the view unfolds.

Antique Spell

Rita Pane describes the magical home she shares with husband Mariano as a "virtual wonderland". A fairytale villa surrounded by an enchanting garden, Villa Tritone on the Amalfi Coast embodies the Riviera fantasy of escaping to a reinvented world. Indeed, Rita sometimes thinks of herself as Alice, who having fallen down the rabbit hole, peers through the keyhole into a secret garden, and does everything in her power to let herself in. This potent image has stayed with her since childhood when she attended the convent school across the road. Each day, she peered through the imposing gates of Villa Tritone, wondering dreamily of what lay behind, never imagining she would one day live there. When the couple finally made the villa their own, shortly after their marriage, they viewed its spectacular sylvan setting as the best gift they could one day give to their children.

Appropriately, the garden has been the focus of much of the couple's attentions. Rita is passionate about gardens and is the author of a book tracing the history of gardens and their meaning: to her they signify a "lost paradise". The history of Villa Tritone itself, however, is one of paradise found. Although the site was once occupied by an ancient Roman villa, built in the first century AD as home to the nephew of Emperor Augustus, its current incarnation is largely the work of William Waldorf Astor. He purchased the site after being smitten by the charms of the Amalfi Coast while on a Grand Tour of Italy at the end of the

♆ LEFT & OPPOSITE The grounds laid out under previous owner William Waldorf Astor mixed a fascination for the aesthetics and motifs of ancient Greece and Imperial Rome with an English passion for gardens and exotic plants. Astor imported and planted hundreds of tropical trees and rare plant varieties.

nineteenth century, and eventually constructed a magnificent house in the belle époque style that was so popular at the time.

A great garden-lover, Waldorf enthusiastically set about transforming the grounds. His neighbour, Princess Maria-Sturdza Cortschacow, cousin of the Russian Tsar, was equally green-fingered and they entered into an informal competition to see who could import the most exotic plants and create the most dramatically manicured garden settings. Astor was apparently considered the winner in the end.

When Rita and Mariano Pane bought the house, it was still full of the furniture which Astor had collected. They made his vision their own by adding antique pieces here and there, and by mixing in some contemporary touches. Astor's presence is still clearly there though, in the vast treasure trove of Roman antiquities — columns, busts, fountains and statues — which still dot the house and grounds. It is in the garden that these stone and marble objects are at their most dramatic, aged by the elements and commanding spectacular views out over Sorrento and the Bay of Naples.

Ψ LEFT & ABOVE Intricately decorated stucco arches and soaring proportions form an impressive setting for a collection of marble columns, archaeological fragments, statues, busts and urns. Some of these pieces were left in the villa by William Waldorf Astor; some have been added by its current owners.

Ψ **LEFT** Unifying the interiors with the magnificent gardens outside is the motif of ancient civilisation — freestanding classical columns, marble bas-reliefs, urns and statuary appear throughout the villa.

OPPOSITE The theme of antiquity continues in the main sitting room with its friezes depicting mythological scenes. Despite these extravagant touches, a colour palette restricted to white with hints of blue creates an overall look of purity. Also making its presence felt is the garden, with potted palms and a centrepiece of exotic cuttings adding a lush note to the decorative scheme.

Riviera Guide

CÔTE D'AZUR

ST TROPEZ

HOTELS
Hotel Byblos
Ave. Paul Signac
tel: 04 94 56 68 00

Chateau de la Messardière
Route de Tahiti
tel: 04 94 56 76 00

Hotel la Sube
15, Quai Suffren 9
tel: 04 94 97 30 04

Bastide de St Tropez
Route des Carles
tel: 04 94 97 58 16

RESTAURANTS
La Ponche
Port des Pêcheurs, Pl. Revelin
tel: 04 94 97 02 53

Bistrot des Lices
3, Pl. des Lices
tel: 04 94 97 28 31

La Cascade
5, rue de l'Eglise
tel: 04 94 54 83 46

L'Olivier
Route des Carles
tel: 04 94 97 58 16

La Marine
22, Quai Jean-Jaurés
tel: 04 94 97 04 07

NIGHTLIFE
Les Caves du Roy
Hotel le Byblos
tel: 04 94 97 16 02

Le Papagayo
St Tropez port
tel: 04 94 97 07 56

JUAN-LES-PINS

HOTELS
Belles Rives
33, Bd. Eduard Baudoin
tel: 04 93 61 02 79

NICE

HOTELS
Hotel Negresco
37, Promenade des Anglais
tel: 04 93 16 64 00

RESTAURANTS
Nissa-Socca
5, Rue Ste. Reparate
tel 04 93 80 18 35

Auberge de Bellet
St Roman de Bellet
629, Route de Bellet
tel: 04 93 37 83 84

Le Comptoir
20, Rue Saint-François-de-Paule
tel: 04 93 92 08 80

St. Jean Cap Ferrat

HOTELS

La Voile d'Or
Yachting harbour
tel: 04 93 01 13 13

Gran Hotel du Cap Ferrat
Bd. Général de Gaulle
tel: 04 93 76 50 50

Brise Marine
58, Ave. Jean Mermoz
tel: 04 93 76 04 36

RESTAURANTS

Le Provençal
2, Ave. Denis Séméria
tel: 04 93 76 03 97

Beaulieu-sur-Mer

HOTELS

La Reserve de Beaulieu
5, Bd. Général Leclerc
tel: 04 93 01 00 01

Le Metropole
15, Bd. Général Leclerc
tel: 04 93 01 00 08

RESTAURANTS

Senzo
Port de Plaisance
tel: 04 93 01 65 75

NIGHTLIFE

Jimmy'Z
Casino Palais des Festivals
Monte Carlo
tel: 04 93 68 00 07

The Italian Riviera

Portofino

HOTELS

Hotel Splendido
Salita Baratta, 13
tel: 0185 269 551
fax: 0185 299614

Splendido Mare
Via Roma
tel: 0185 269 551
fax: 0185 269614

RESTAURANTS

Piiosforo
Molo Umberto I, 9
tel: 0185 269020

Stella
Molo Umberto I, 3
tel: 0185 269007

Antica Osteria del Carugio
Via Cappellini, 66
tel: 0187 900617

NIGHTLIFE

Carillon
Via Paraggi a Mare, 10
Santa Margherita Ligure
tel: 0185 286721

Forte Dei Marmi

HOTELS

Augustus
Viale Morin, 169
tel: 0584 787200

Franceschi
Via XX Settembre
tel: 0584 787114

Pensione Bandinelli
Via Torino, 3
tel: 0584 787455

BAGNI & RESTAURANTS

Bagno Piero
Via Arenile, 1
tel: 0584 81647

Bagno America
Via della Repubblica, 4
tel: 0584 83996

Orsa Maggiore
Via della Repubblica, 29
tel: 0584 82219

Maitó
Via Arenile, 28
tel: 0584 80940

Da Valé
Piazza Garibaldi, 4
tel: 0584 89361

NIGHTLIFE
La Capannina di Santini Gianluca
Via della Repubblica, 18
0584 83414

La Canniccia
Località Marina di Pietrosanta
Via Unitá d'Italia, 1
Fiumetto
tel: 0584 23225

PORTO ERCOLE &
MONTE ARGENTARIO

HOTELS
Il Pellicano
Porto Ercole
tel: 0564 858111

Don Pedro
Via Panoramica, 7
Porto Ercole
tel: 0564 833914

Filippo II
Località Poggio Calvello
tel: 0564 812694

Torre di Cala Piccola
Località Cala Piccola
tel: 0564 825144

Terme di Saturnia
Località Saturnia
tel: 0564 601061

Locanda Laudomia
Località Poderi di Monte Merano
tel: 0564 620013

NIGHTLIFE
La Strega del Mare
Località Cala Grande
tel: 0564 824191

RESTAURANTS
Da Armando
Via Marconi, 2
Porto Santo Stefano
tel: 0564 822568

King's Bar and Restaurant
Lungomare Andrea Doria
Porto Ercole
tel: 0564 831007

Il Gambero Rosso
Lungomare Andrea Doria
Porto Ercole
tel: 0564 832650

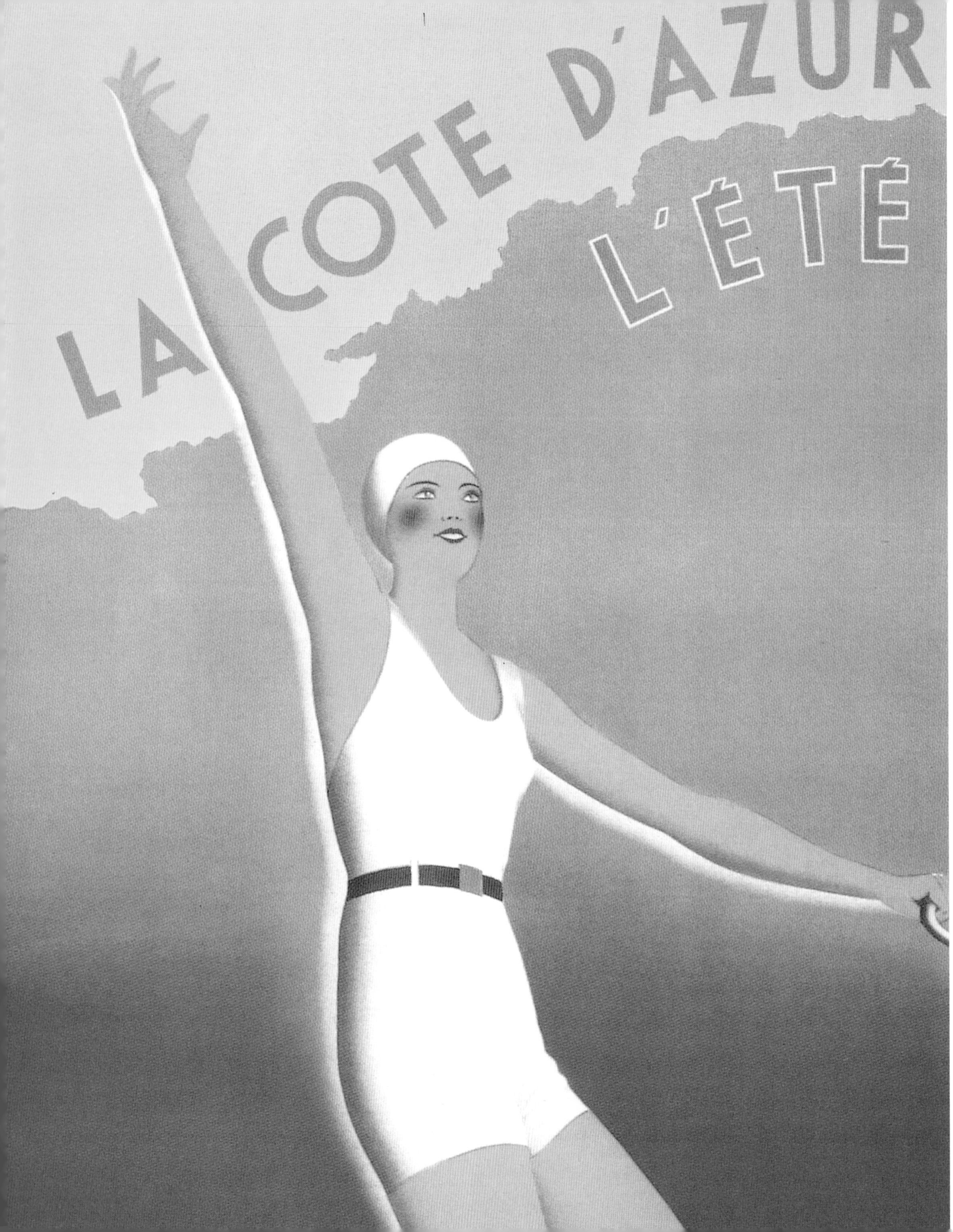
LA COTE D'AZUR
L'ÉTÉ

La Fontanina
Località San Pietro
tel: 0564 825261

Locanda di Ansedornia
Via Aurelia Km 140-500
Orbetello
tel: 0564 881717

Pitorsino
Via Aurelia Km 140
Orbetello
tel: 0564 86279

CAPRI & THE AMALFI COAST

CAPRI

HOTELS

Hotel Quisisana
Via Camerelle, 2
tel: 081 8370788

La Scalinatella
Via Tragara, 8–10
tel: 081 8370633
fax: 081 8378291

BEACH RESTAURANTS

La Canzone del Mare
Via Marina Piccola, 93
tel: 081 8370104

Da Luigi
Via Faraglioni
tel: 081 8370845

RESTAURANTS

La Capannina
Via delle Botteghe, 14
tel: 081 8370732

Da Paolino
Via Palazzo a Mare, 11
tel: 081 8376102

Le Grottelle
Via Matermania, 3
tel: 081 8375719

NIGHTLIFE

Anema & Core
Via Sella Orta, 1
tel: 081 8376461

Pentothal
Via V. Emanuele, 45
tel: 081 8376793

SORRENTO

HOTELS

Hotel Bellevue Syrene
Piazza della Vittoria, 5
tel: 081 8781024

Sant' Angelo
Pl. dei Capi
Cocumello
tel: 081 8793042

RESTAURANTS

Don Alfonso 1890
Sant' Agata sui due Golfi, 11
tel: 081 8780026

POSITANO

HOTELS

La Sirenuse
Via C. Colombo, 30
tel 089 875001

San Pietro
Via Laurito, 2
tel: 089 875455

Palazzo Murat
Via dei Mulini, 23
tel: 089 875177

RESTAURANTS

La Buca di Bacco
Via Rampa Teglia, 4
tel: 089 875699

La Cambusa
Piamma Amerigo Vespucci
tel: 089 875432

Carlo e Tanina
Via Montepertuso Petsella, 69
tel: 089 811806

INDEX

Note: references in *italics* are to captions.

acknowledgments

For their invaluable assistance the publishers gratefully thank: Marchesa Laura Mansi, Isabella Vincenzini, Piera and Antonio Fontana, Giulia Boroli, Baron and Baroness Casana, Emma Bini Valdoni, Patrizia Campione, Giovanni Russo, Stephen White. Special thanks to all those who kindly allowed their homes to be photographed. The publishers extend sincere apologies to those whose homes could not be included in the book due to space constraints.